Journaling is a place where you can travel through life's emotions with gentleness, compassion, and deeper understanding.

_____

_____

_____

_____

_____

_____

_____

_____

_____

_____

_____

_____

_____

_____

_____

_____

_____

_____

_____

_____

_____

_____

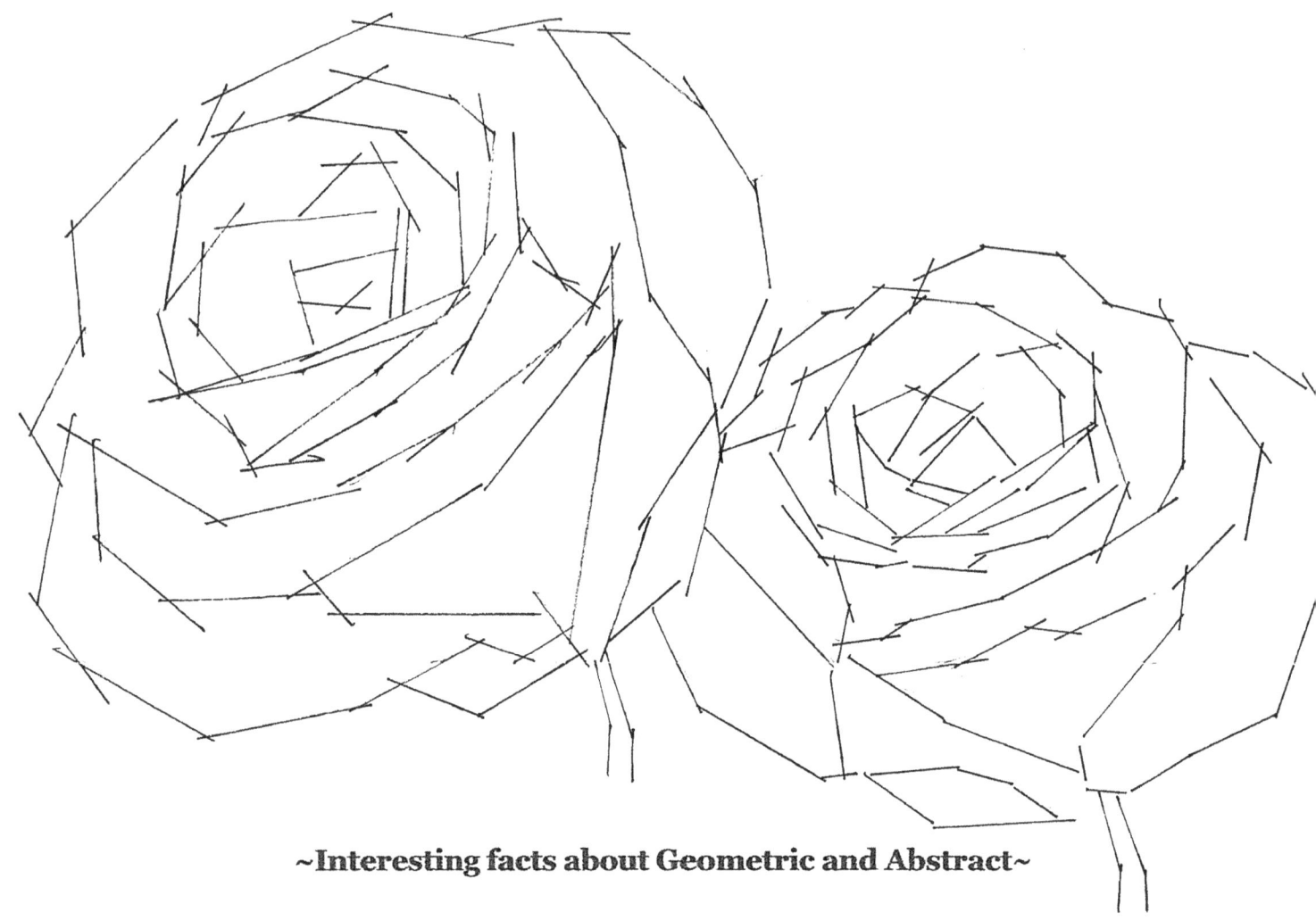

~Interesting facts about Geometric and Abstract~

The word Geometry comes from the Greek words "geo" meaning earth, and "metria". meaning measure.

Ancient Egyptians used geometry principles as far back as 3000 BC.

A Greek mathematician named Euclid who lived around the year 300 BC is often referred to as the "Father of Geometry."

Greeks constructed aesthetically pleasing buildings and works of art based on the golden ratio.

The internal angles of a square add to 360 degrees,

A square has 4 lines of reflectional symmetry.

Triangle shapes are often used in construction because of their great strength.

Plane Geometry is about flat shapes like circles and triangles...shapes that can be drawn on a piece of paper.

A Ploygon is a 2-dimensional shape made of straight lines, like triangles and rectangles.

Journaling is an outlet for processing emotions and increasing self-awareness.

_____

_____

_____

_____

_____

_____

_____

_____

_____

_____

_____

_____

_____

_____

_____

_____

_____

_____

_____

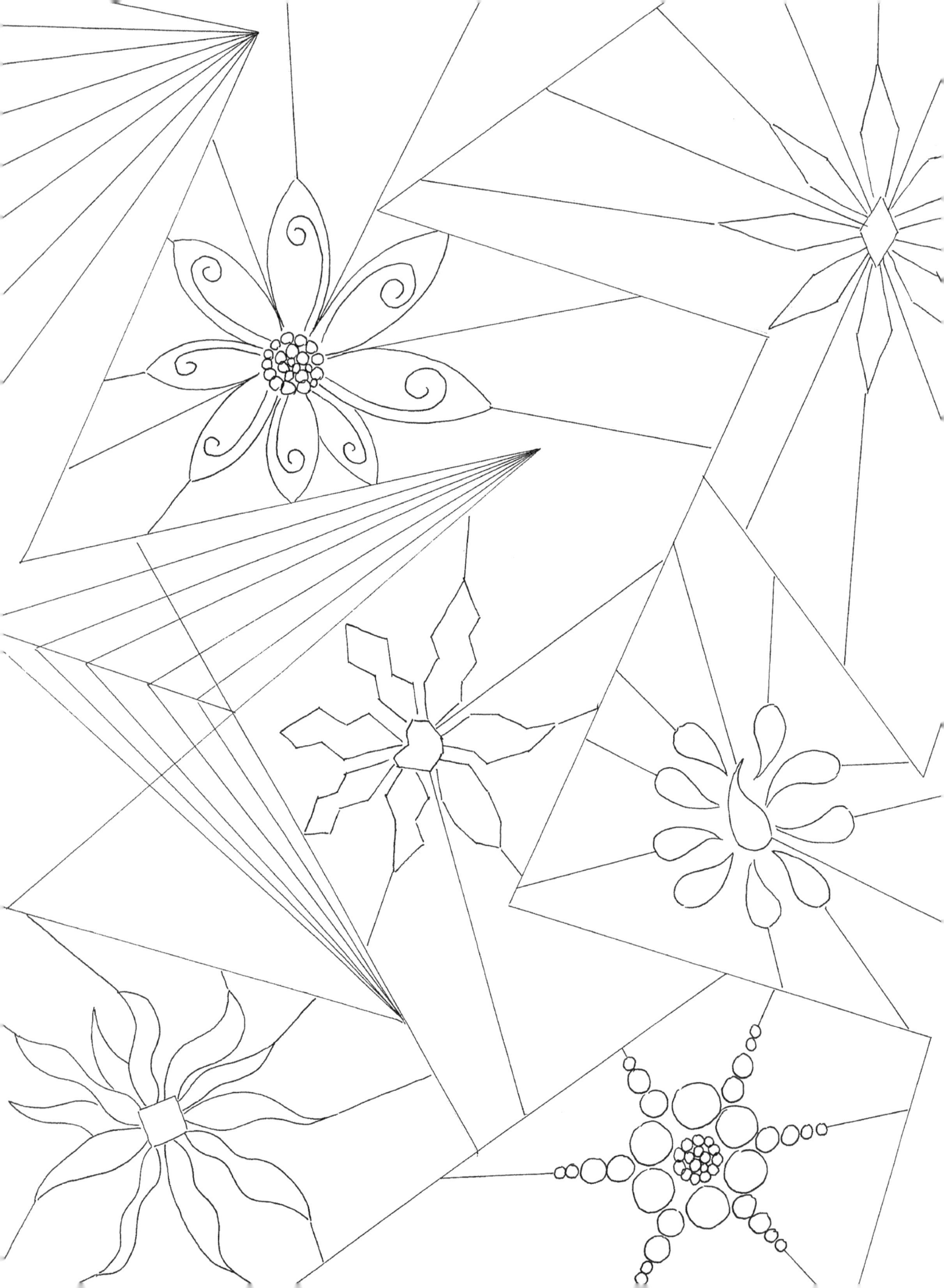

Journaling can include your dreams and ambitions.

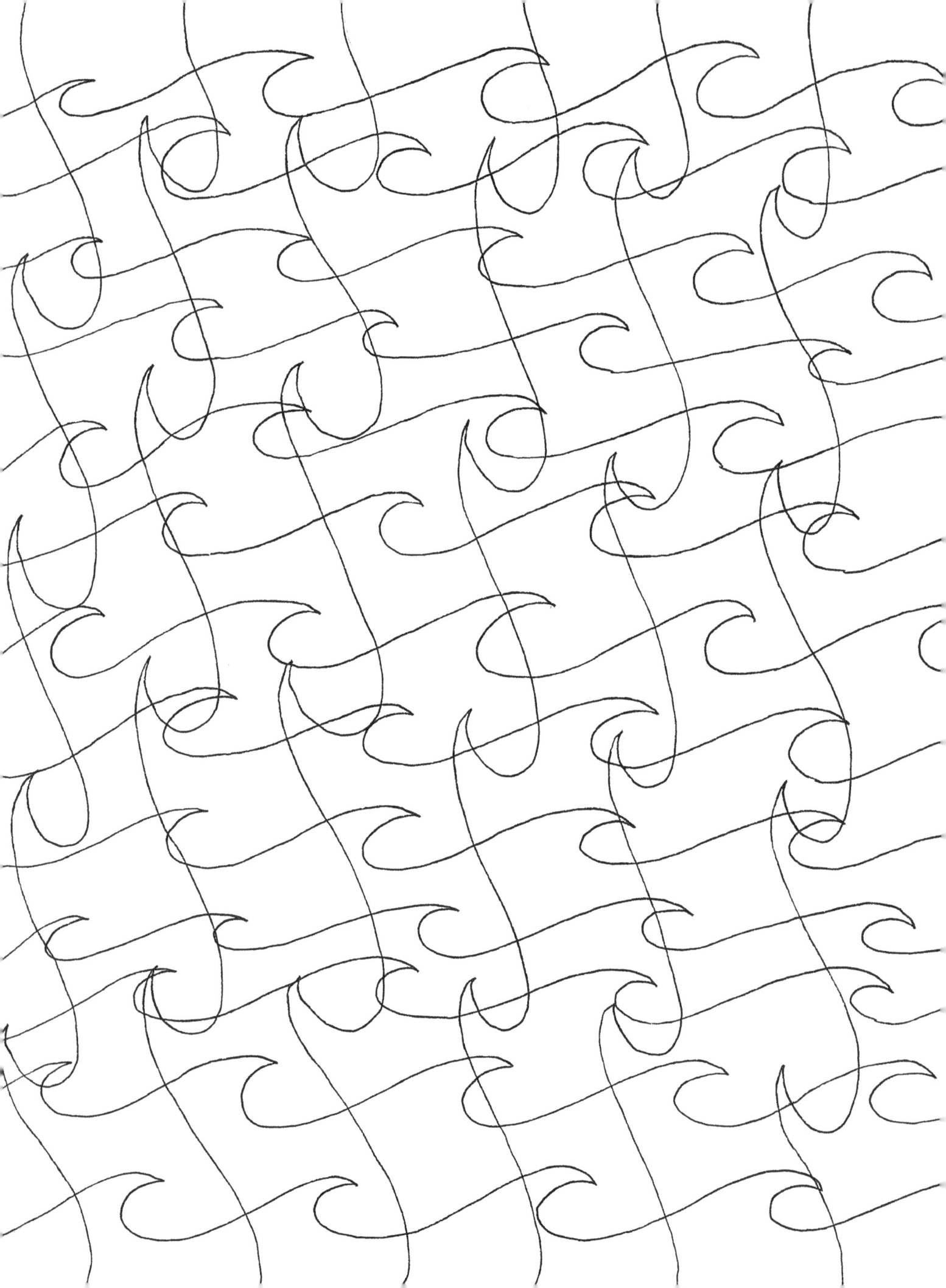

Journaling brings you into a state of mindfulness.

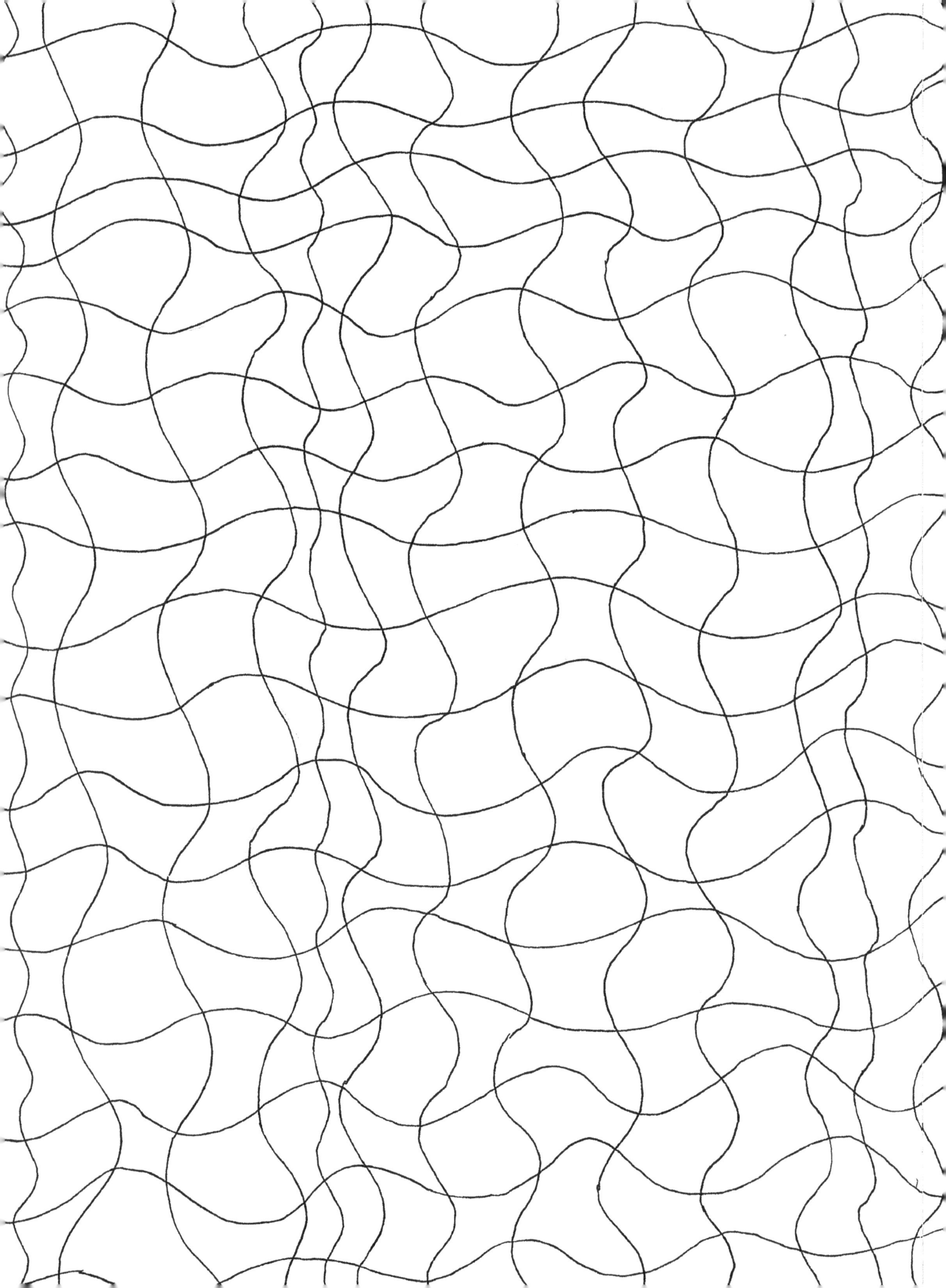

Journaling will stretch your IQ and make you smarter.

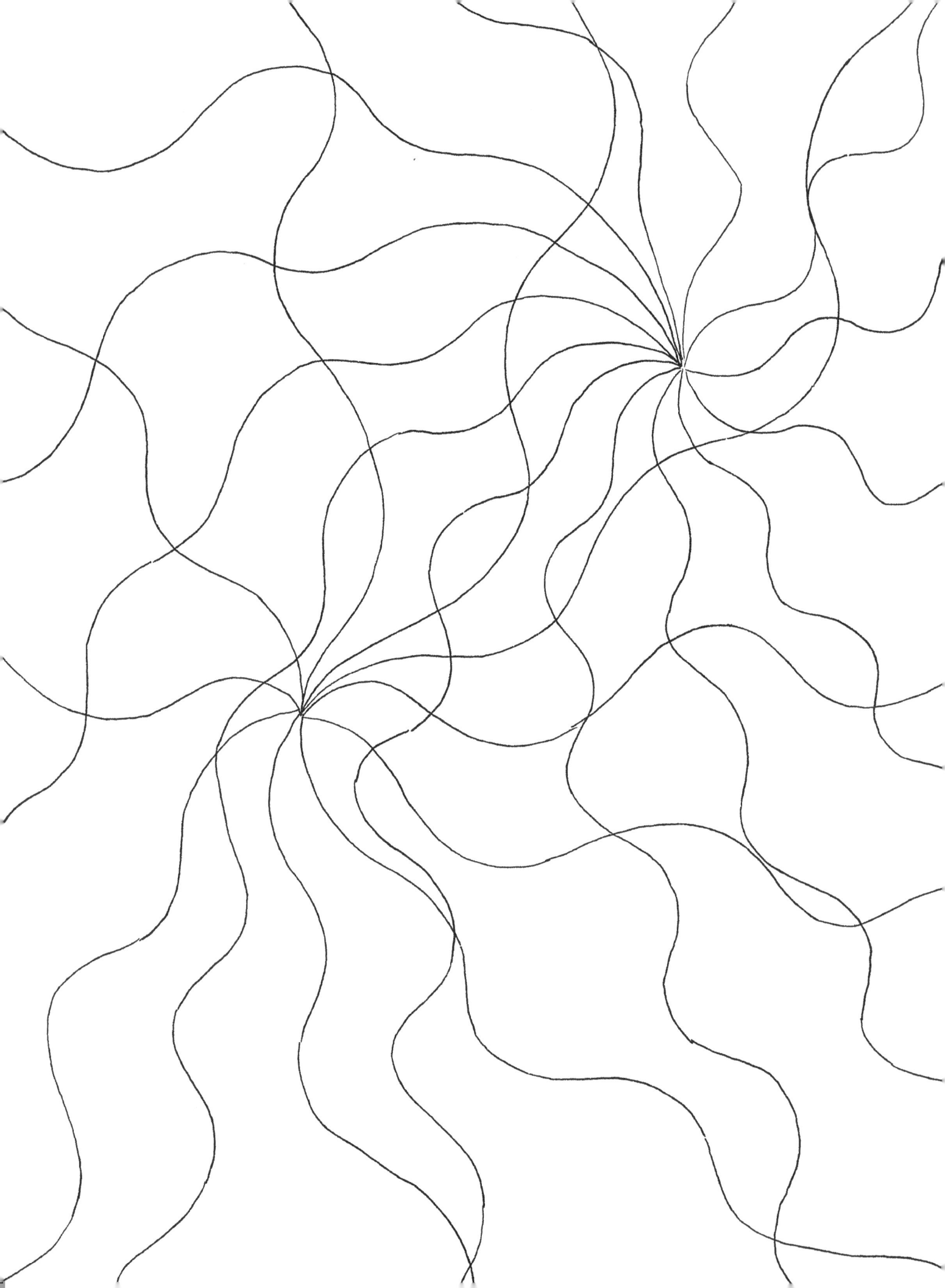

Journaling allows you to track patterns, trends and improvement and growth over time.

_____

_____
_____
_____
_____
_____
_____
_____
_____
_____
_____
_____
_____
_____
_____
_____
_____
_____
_____

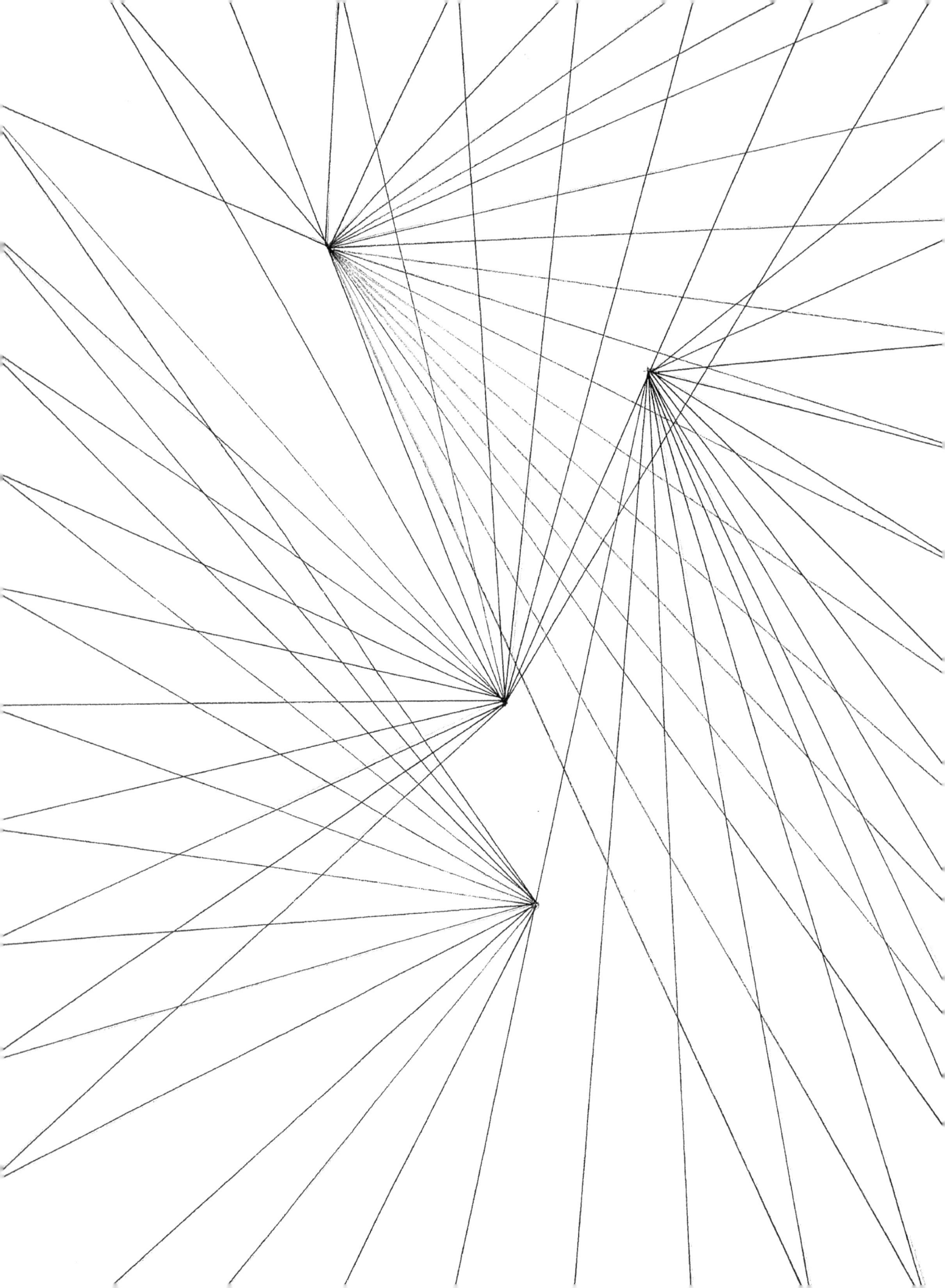

Writing removes mental blocks and allows you to use all your brainpower to better understand yourself, others and the world around you.

_____

_____

_____

_____

_____

_____

_____

_____

_____

_____

_____

_____

_____

_____

_____

_____

_____

_____

_____

_____

_____

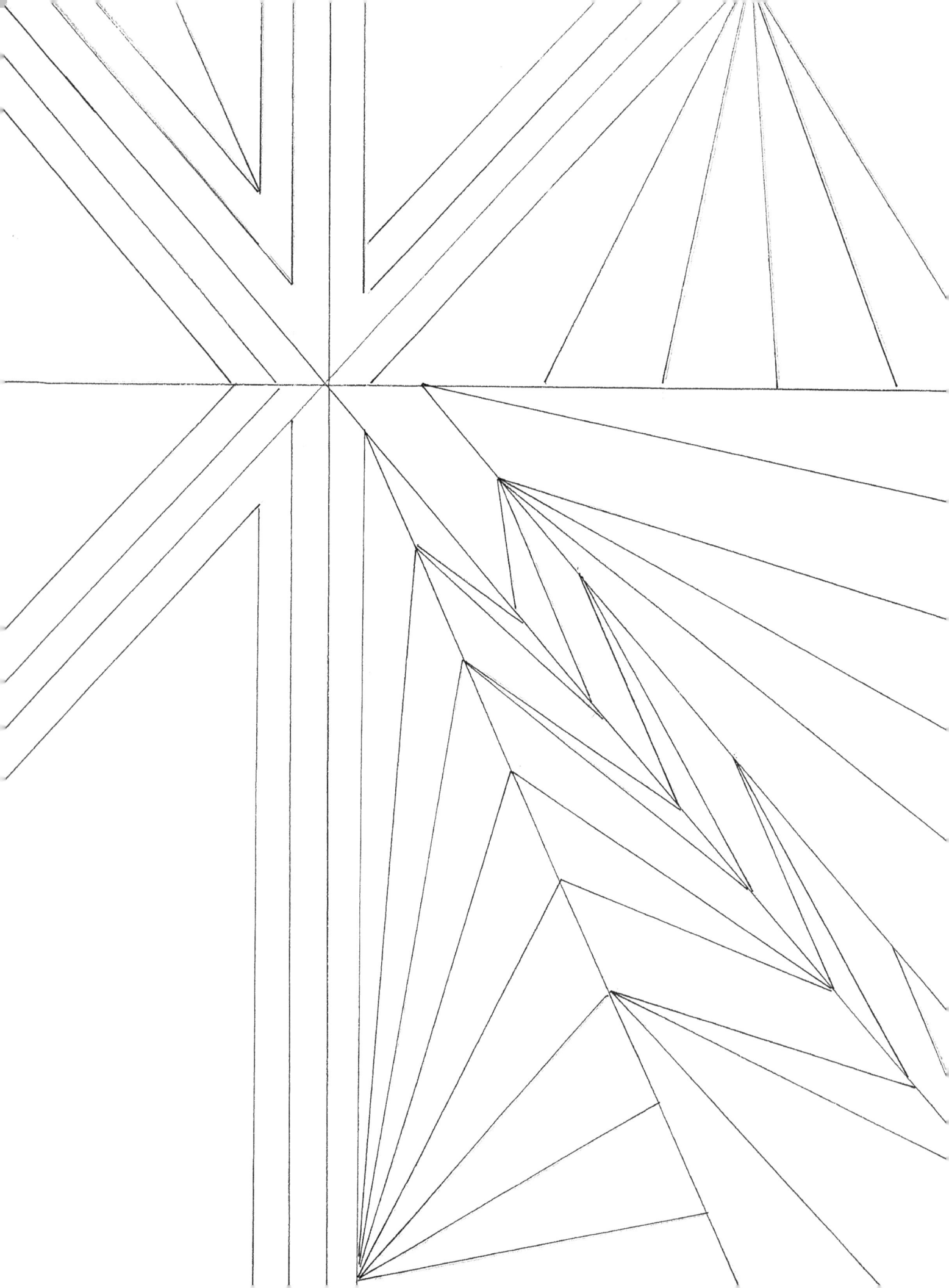

Journaling decreases the symptoms of asthma and rheumatoid arthritis.

_____

_____

_____

_____

_____

_____

_____

_____

_____

_____

_____

_____

_____

_____

_____

_____

_____

_____

_____

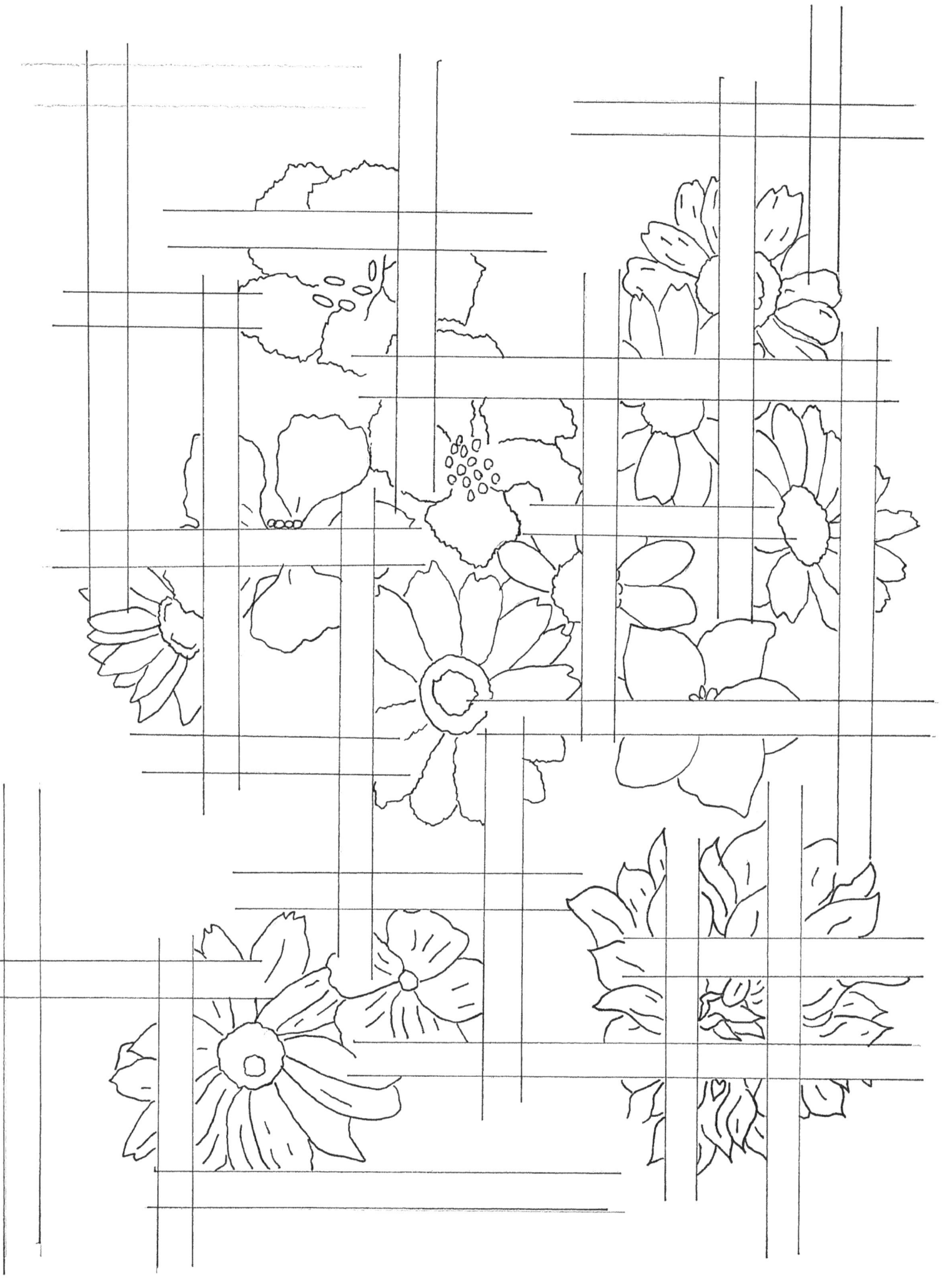

Regular journaling strengthens immune cells, called T-lymphocytes.

_____

_____

_____

_____

_____

_____

_____

_____

_____

_____

_____

_____

_____

_____

_____

_____

_____

_____

_____

_____

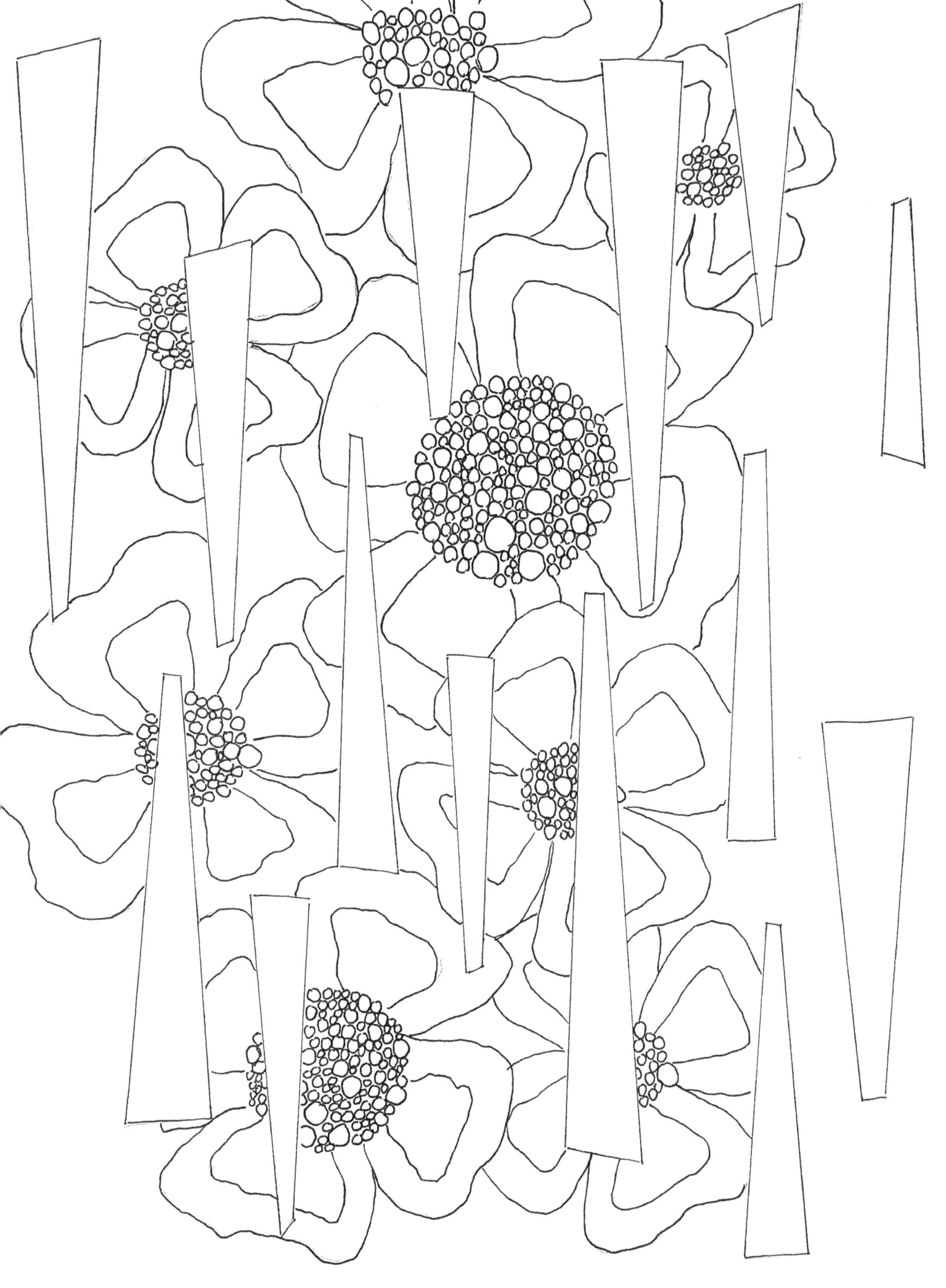

A Pen coupled with paper can serve as a powerful tool.

_____

_____

_____

_____

_____

_____

_____

_____

_____

_____

_____

_____

_____

_____

_____

_____

_____

_____

_____

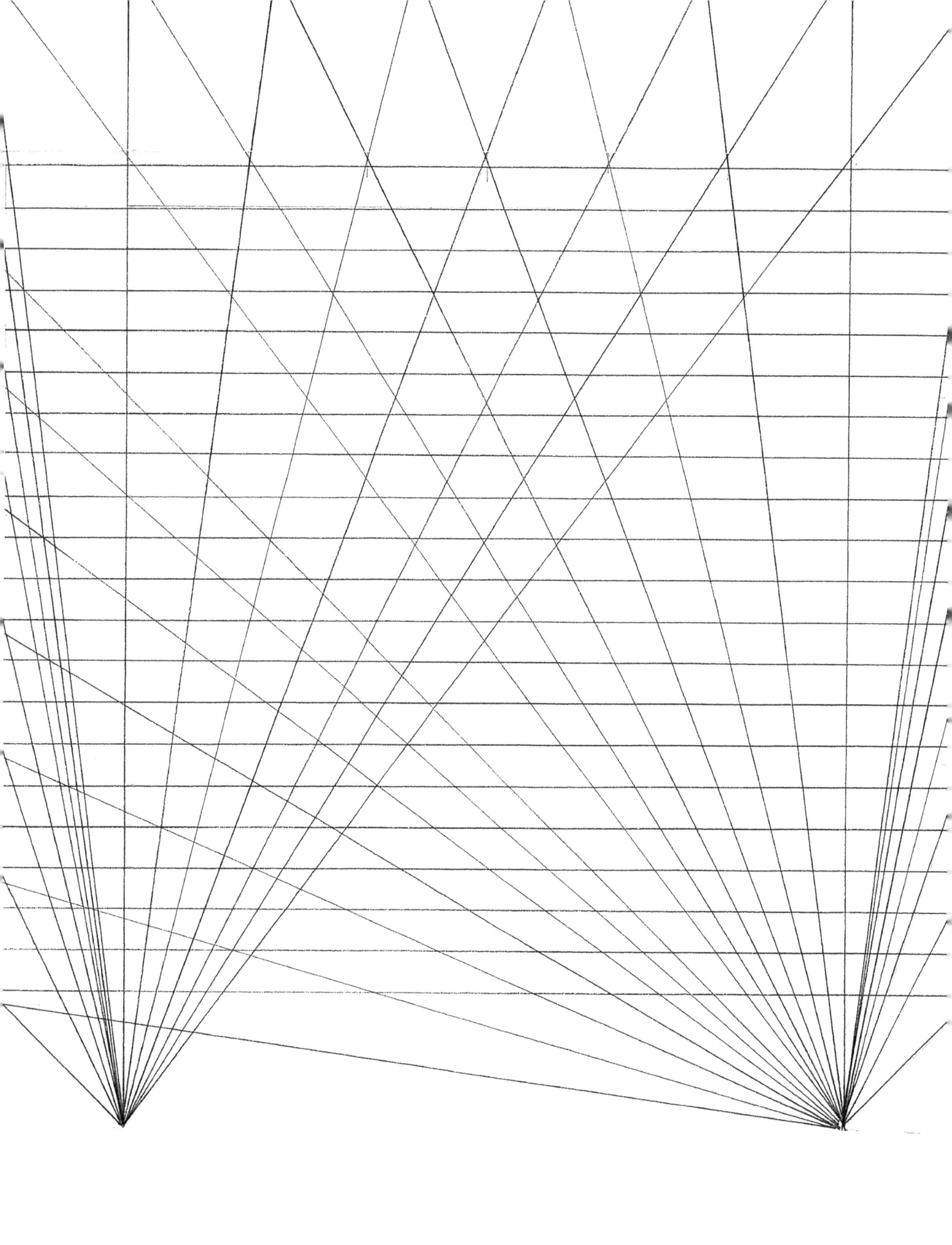

Journaling has a positive impact on physical well-being.

_____

_____

_____

_____

_____

_____

_____

_____

_____

_____

_____

_____

_____

_____

_____

_____

_____

_____

_____

_____

_____

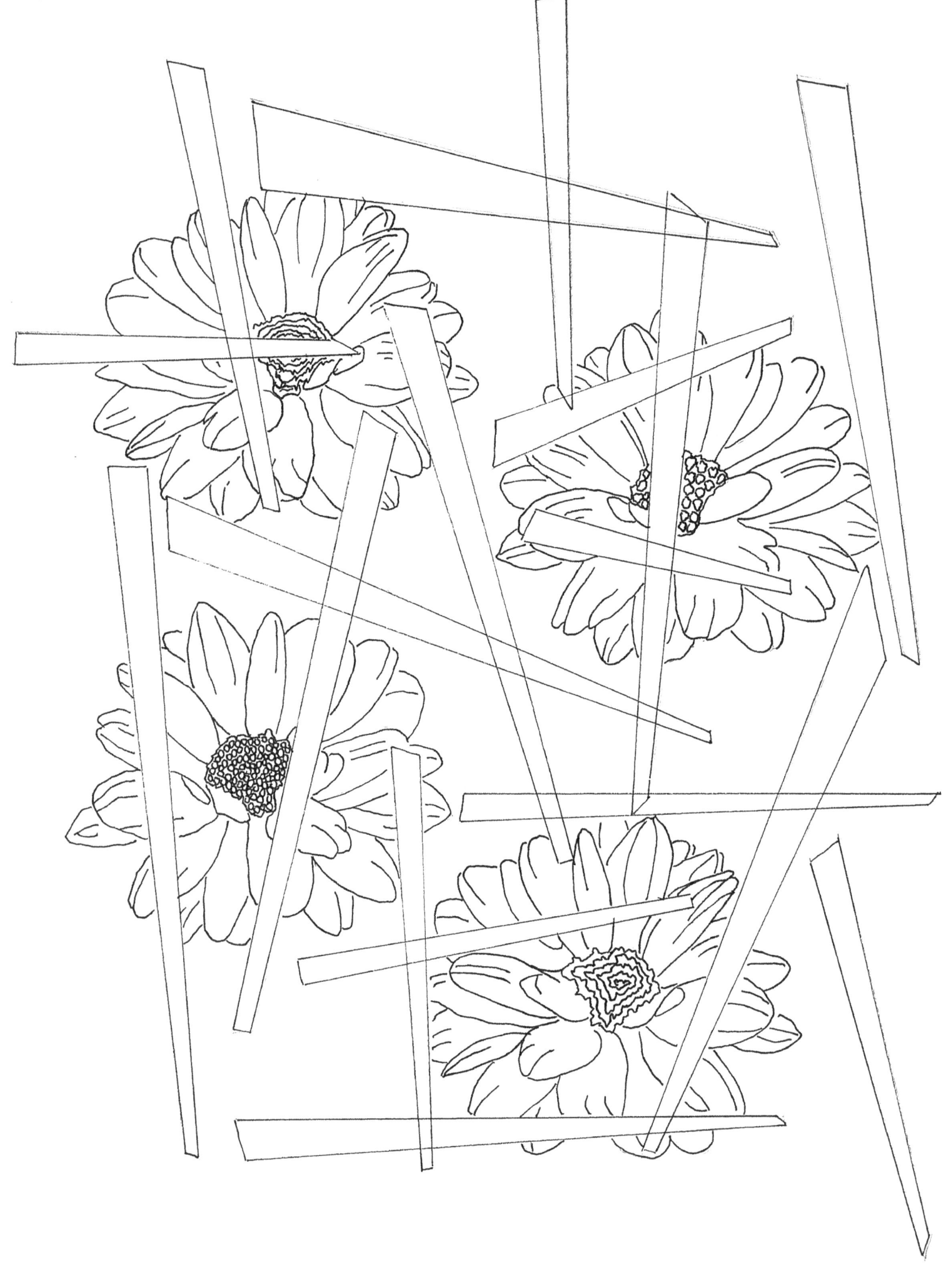

There are never any rules to journaling.

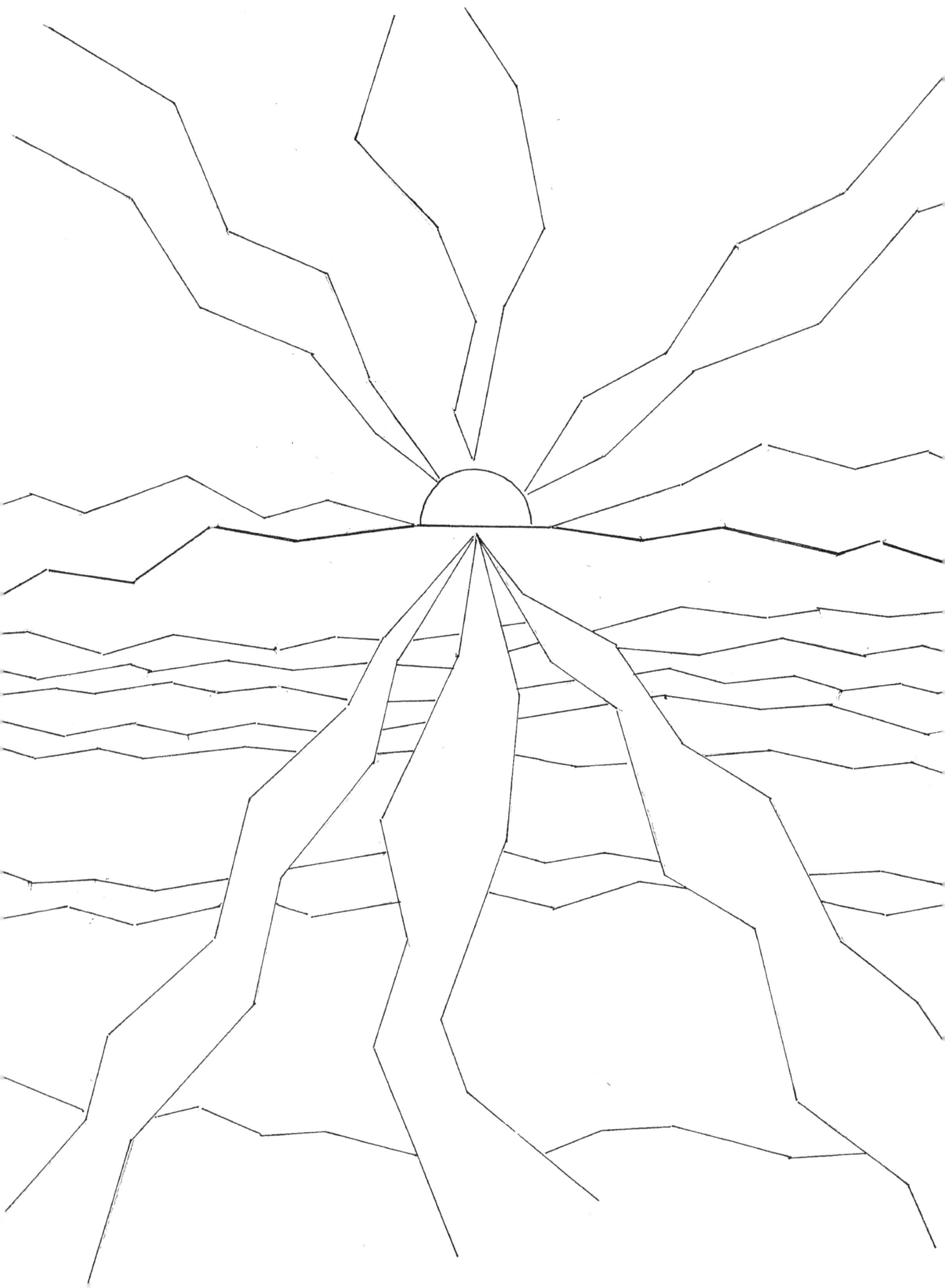

Journaling dates back to at least 10th century Japan.

_____

_____

_____

_____

_____

_____

_____

_____

_____

_____

_____

_____

_____

_____

_____

_____

_____

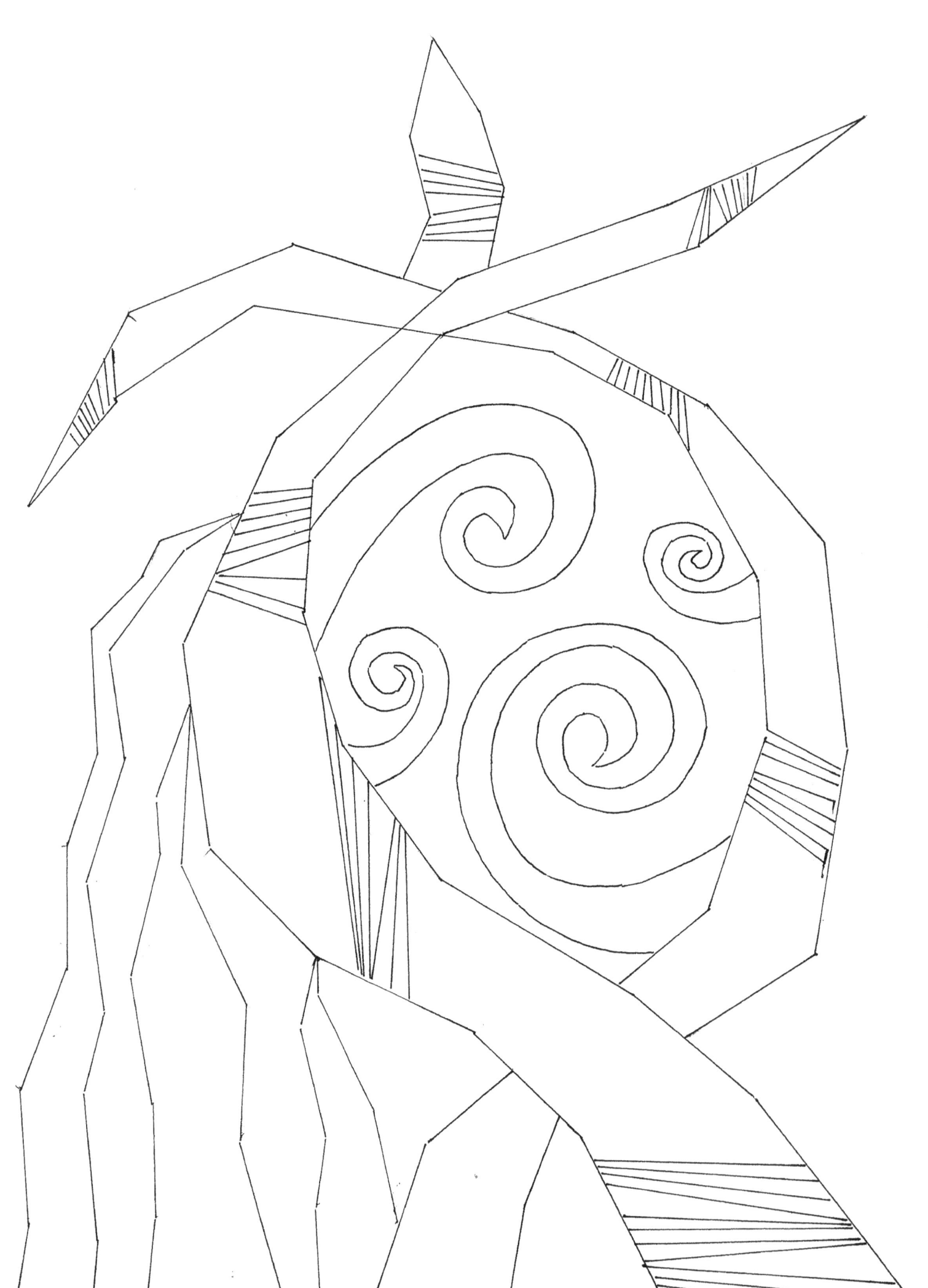

Successful people throughout history have kept journals.

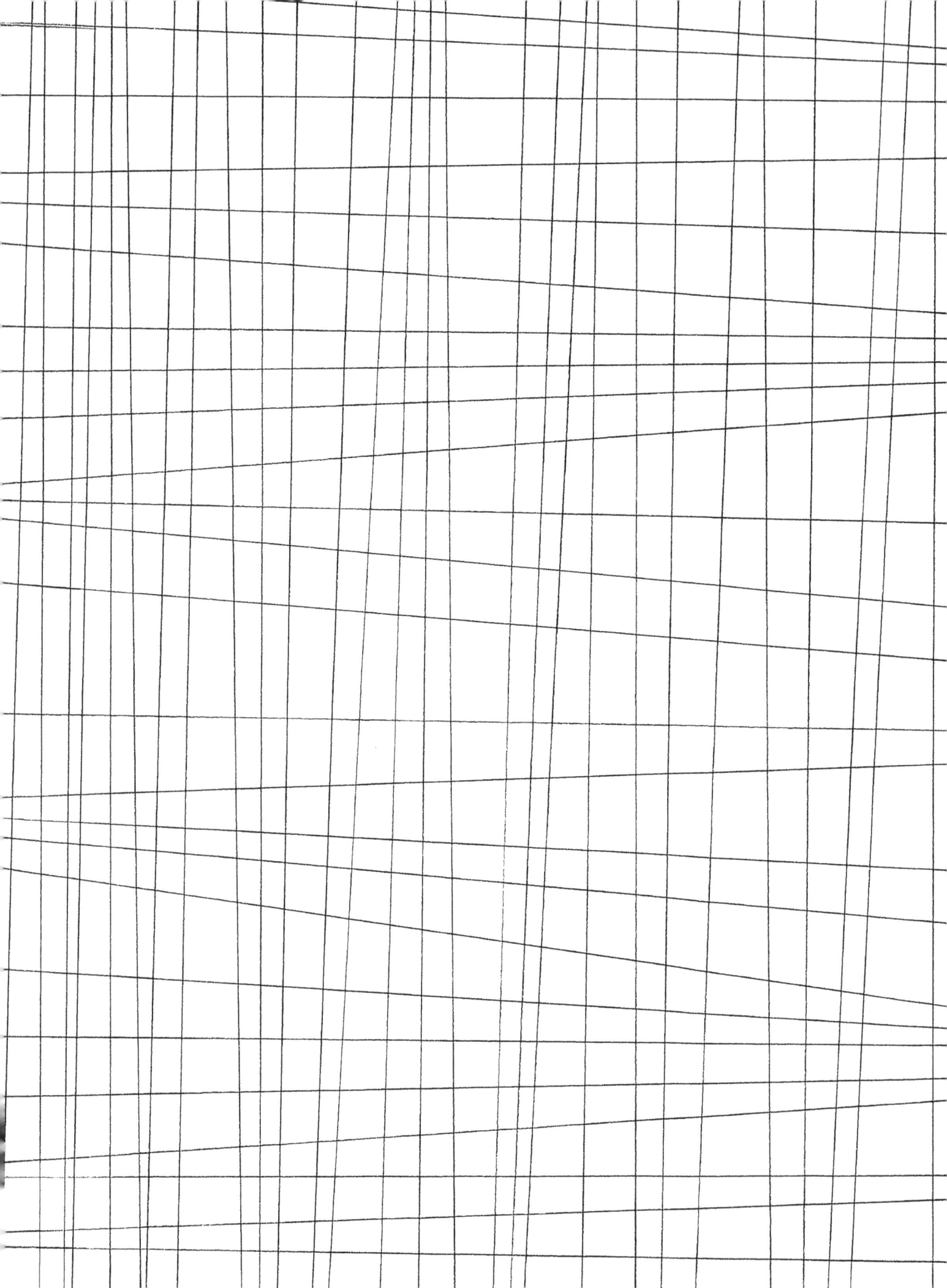

Journals are excellent ways to work through the "hard stuff" like, venting your troubles, emotional distresses

_____

_____

_____

_____

_____

_____

_____

_____

_____

_____

_____

_____

_____

_____

_____

_____

_____

_____

_____

_____

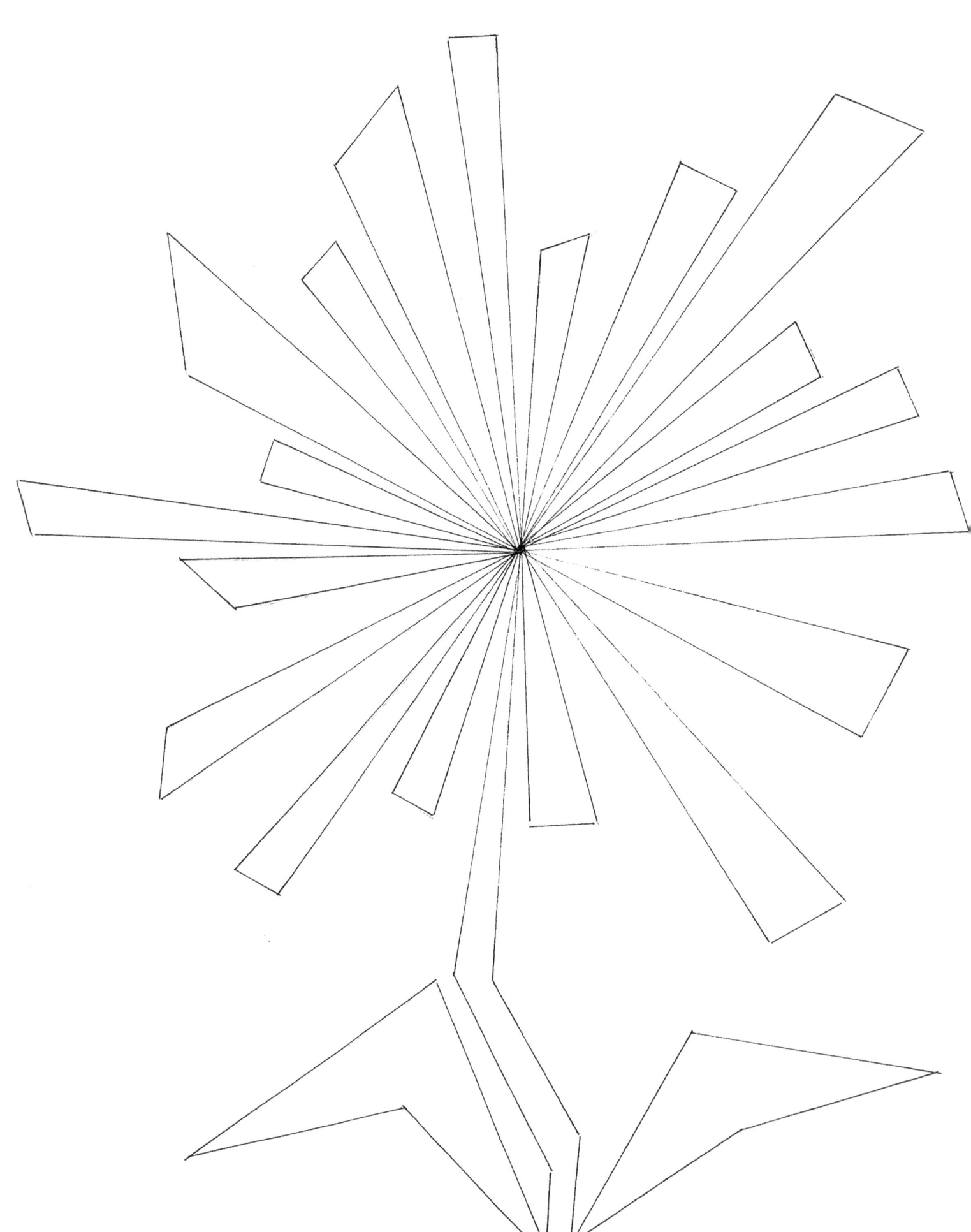

A journal soaks up anger, rage, vengeance, jealousy, a whole plethora of negative emotions and never judges or shout back at you.

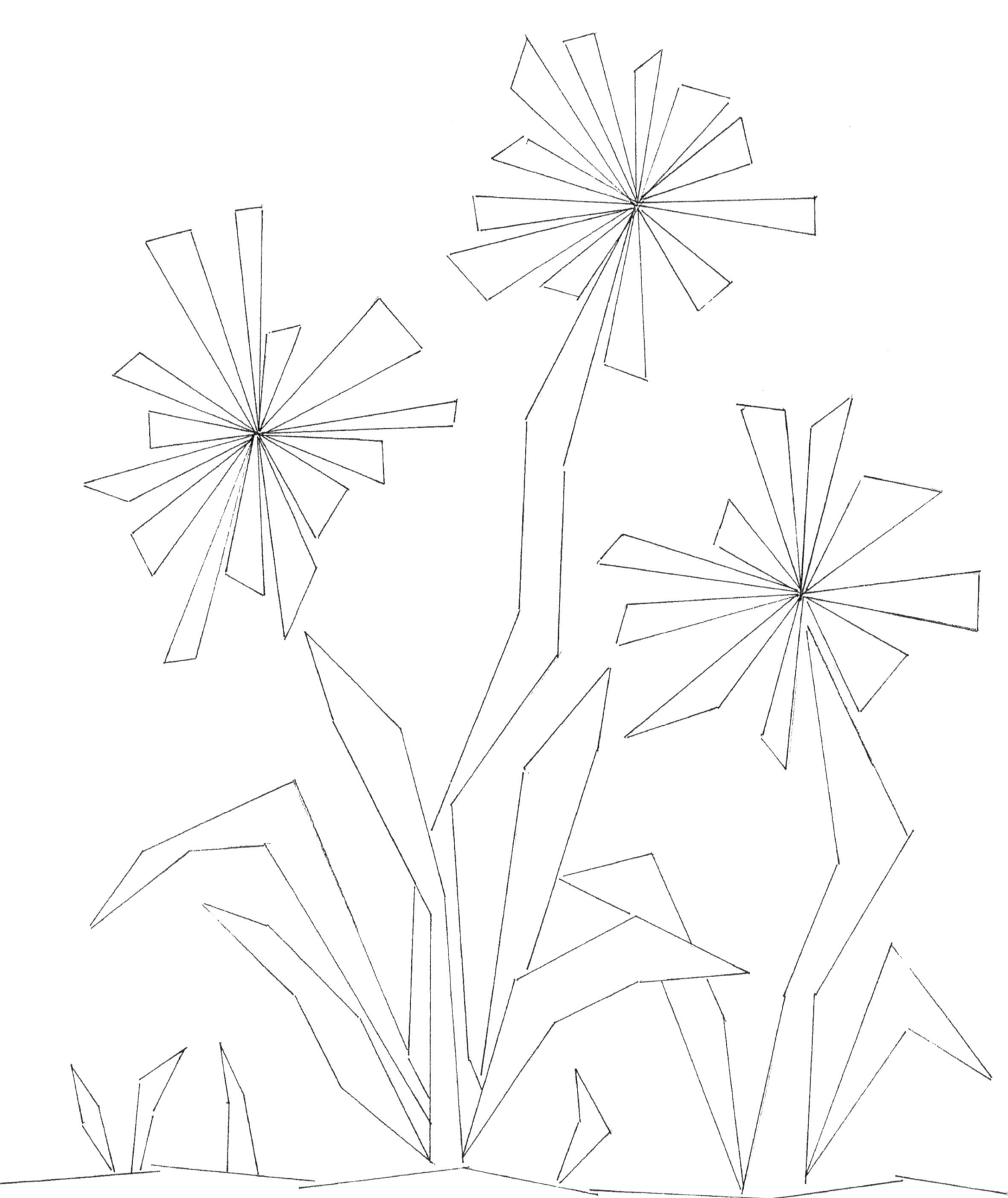

Every person differs in what helps them to relax and feel contented. Colring and writing go hand in hand!

_____

_____

_____

_____

_____

_____

_____

_____

_____

_____

_____

_____

_____

_____

_____

_____

_____

_____

_____

_____

_____

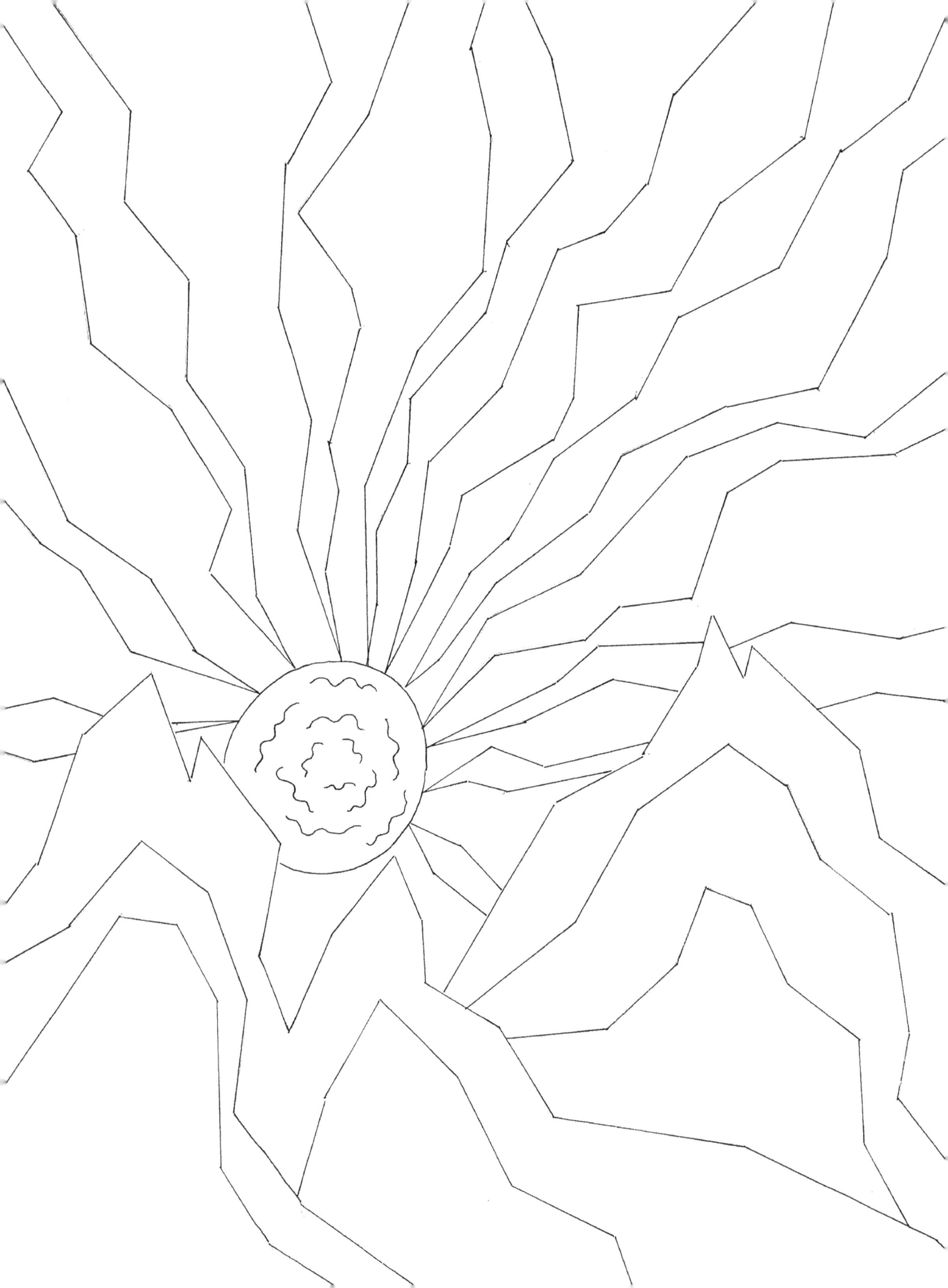

A journal can be full of inspiration you have found from reading, conversing with your girlfriends, watching a movie or going out on a date.

_____

_____

_____

_____

_____

_____

_____

_____

_____

_____

_____

_____

_____

_____

_____

_____

_____

_____

_____

_____

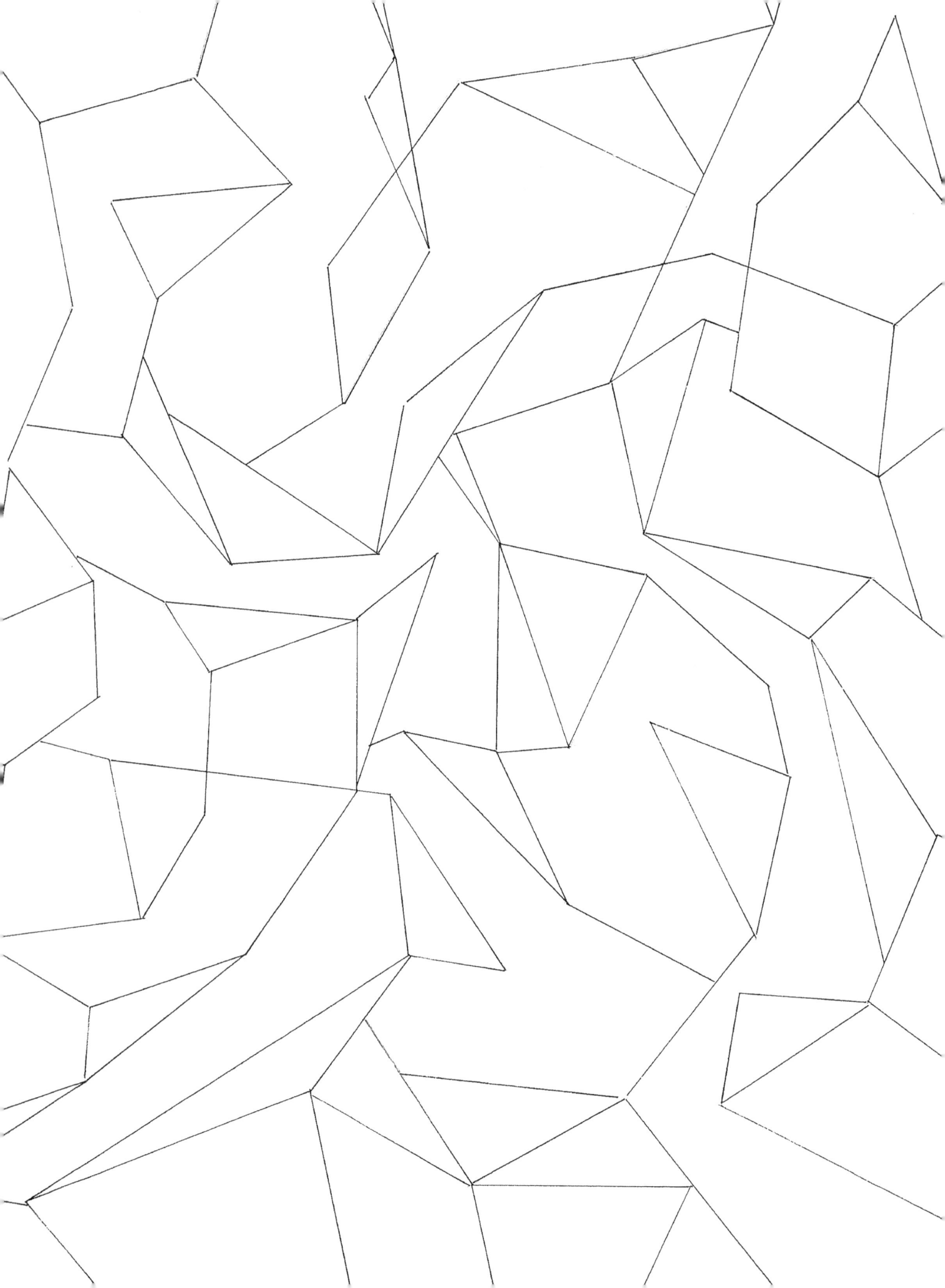

Journals are a great place to collect phrases, sayings, comments, quotes and notes from the world of life.

_____

_____

_____

_____

_____

_____

_____

_____

_____

_____

_____

_____

_____

_____

_____

_____

_____

_____

_____

_____

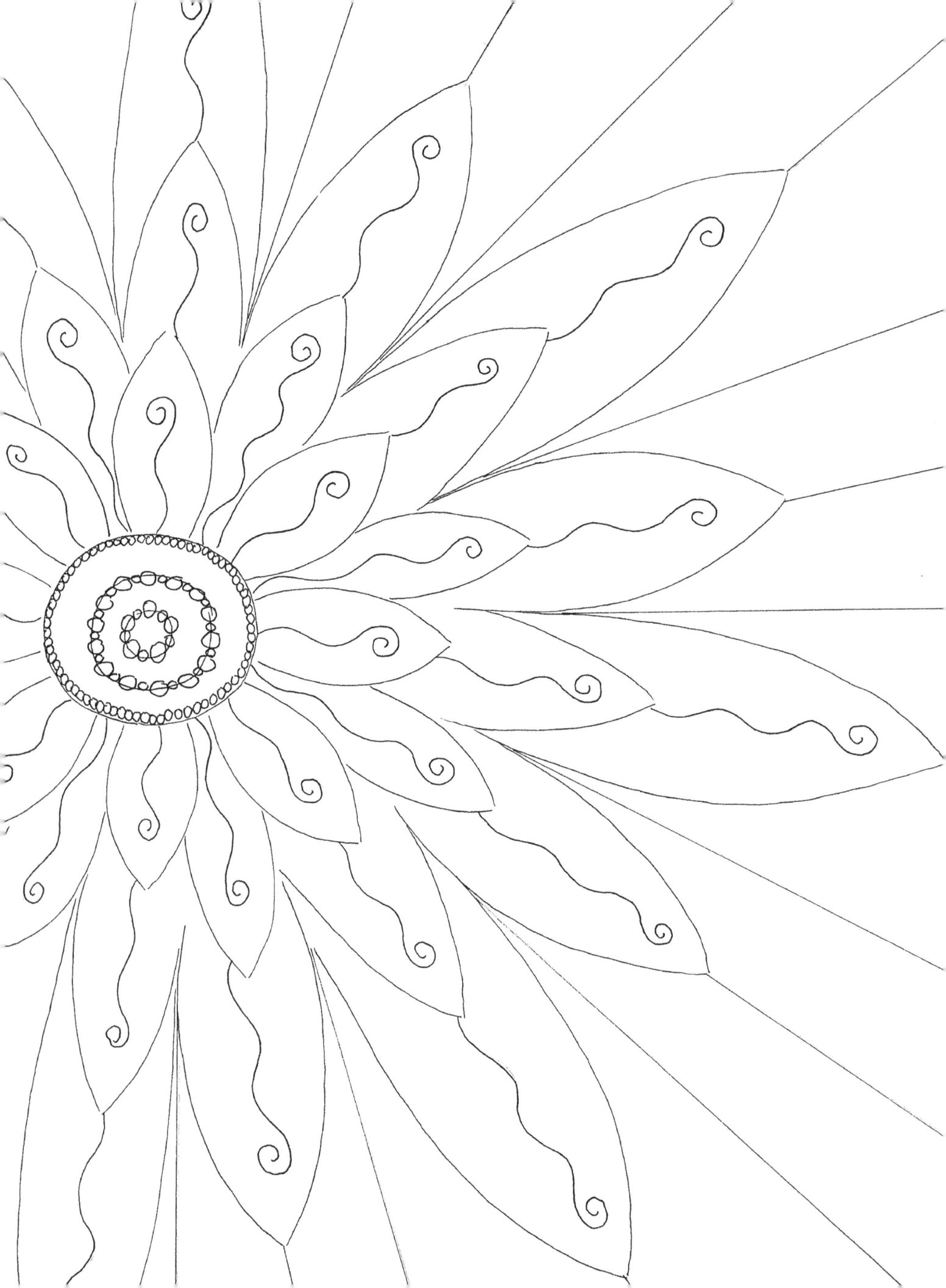

Journaling is about reflection and solitude.

_____

_____

_____

_____

_____

_____

_____

_____

_____

_____

_____

_____

_____

_____

_____

_____

_____

_____

_____

_____

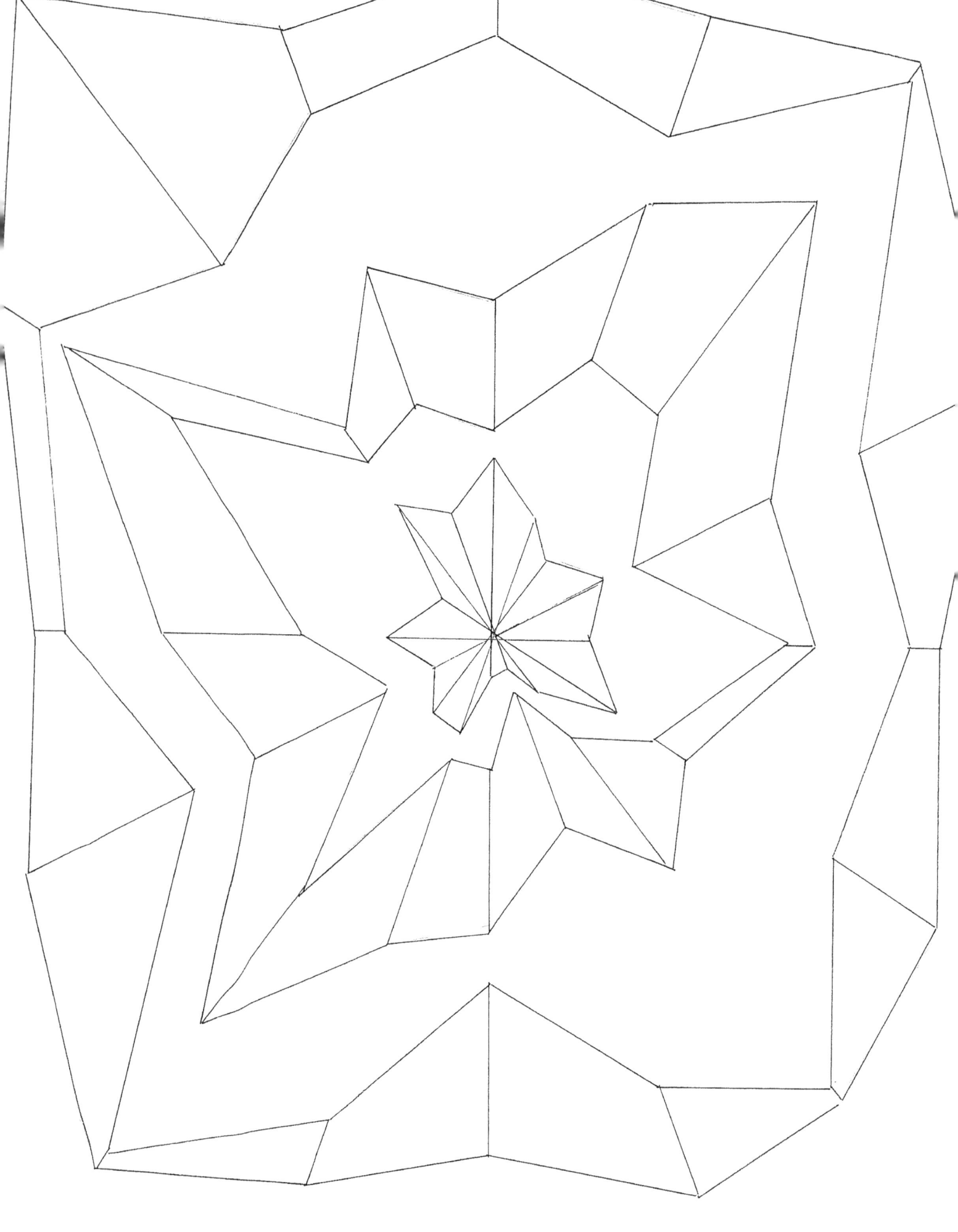

A transition journal is a record of any transition you are going through, such as a job, or the loss of, becoming a parent, starting a business, or a new stage of life you are entering.

_____

_____

_____

_____

_____

_____

_____

_____

_____

_____

_____

_____

_____

_____

_____

_____

_____

_____

_____

_____

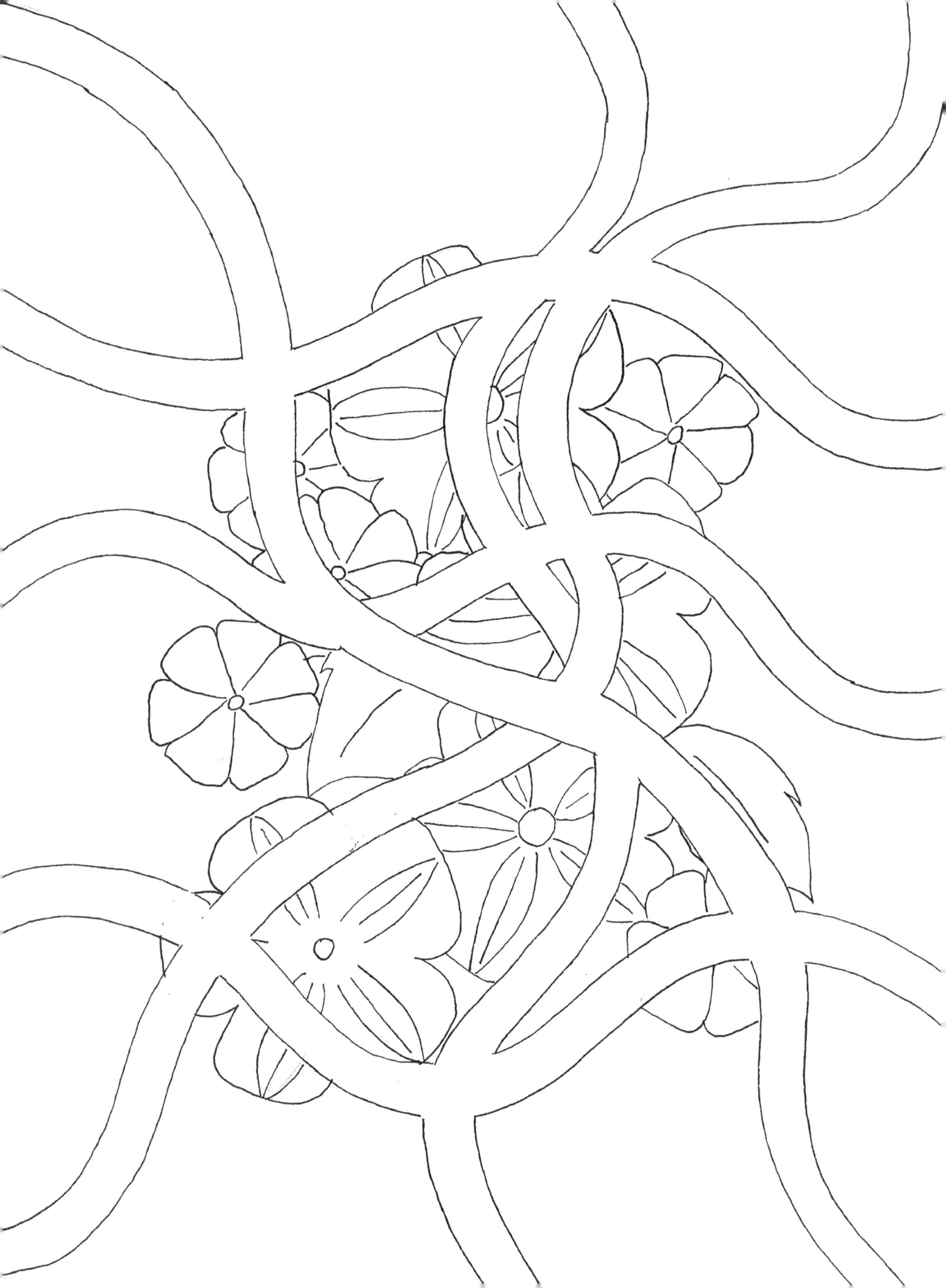

A child journal can include all the things that you feel are special, wonderful, lovable, and memorable about your kids or grandkids at different ages and stages of life.

_____
_____
_____
_____
_____
_____
_____
_____
_____
_____
_____
_____
_____
_____
_____
_____
_____
_____
_____
_____
_____
_____
_____
_____
_____
_____
_____
_____
_____
_____
_____
_____
_____

www.ingramcontent.com/pod-product-compliance
Lightning Source LLC
Chambersburg PA
CBHW081133180526
45170CB00008B/3095

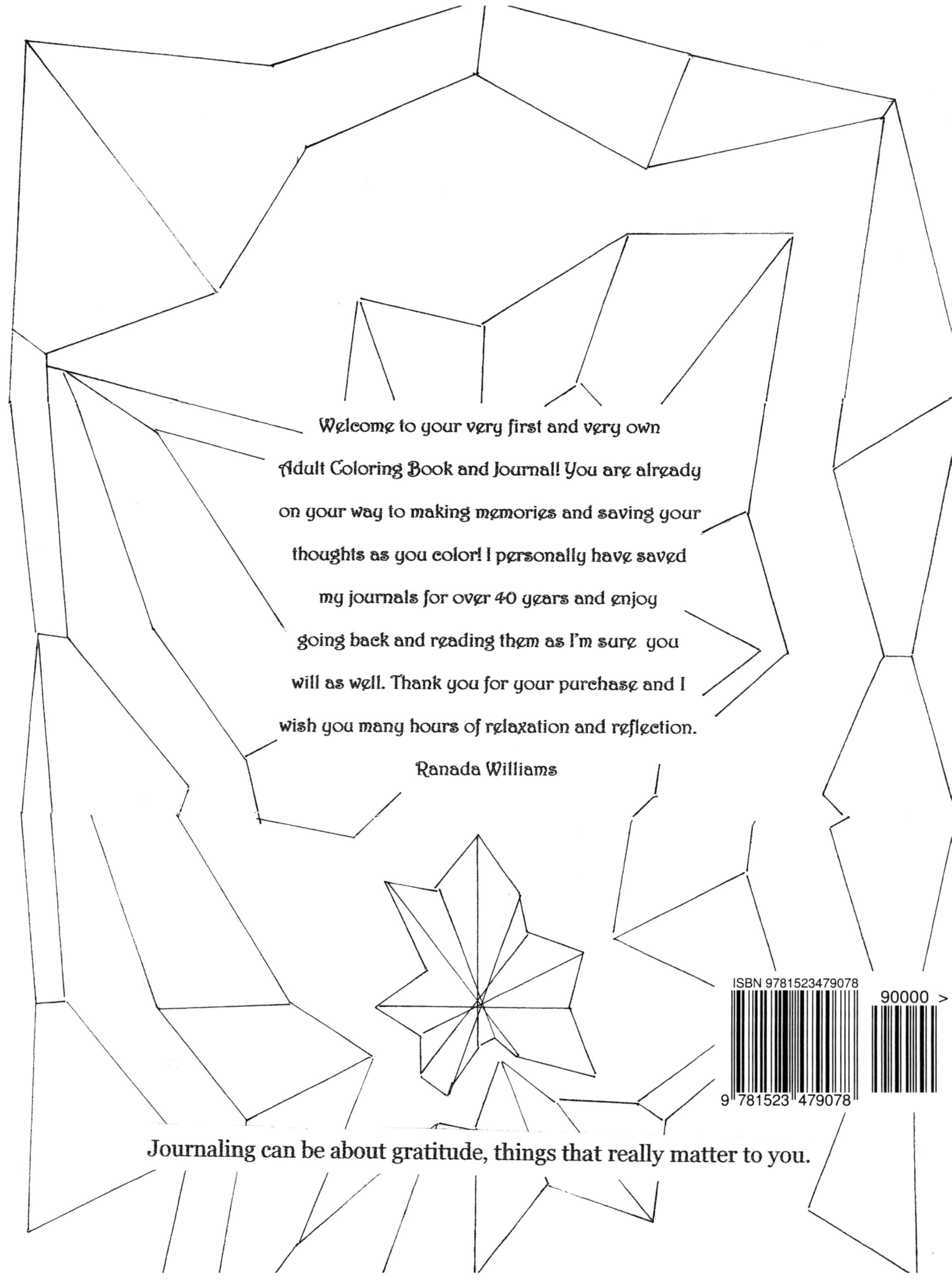

Welcome to your very first and very own
Adult Coloring Book and Journal! You are already
on your way to making memories and saving your
thoughts as you color! I personally have saved
my journals for over 40 years and enjoy
going back and reading them as I'm sure you
will as well. Thank you for your purchase and I
wish you many hours of relaxation and reflection.

Ranada Williams

ISBN 9781523479078

Journaling can be about gratitude, things that really matter to you.

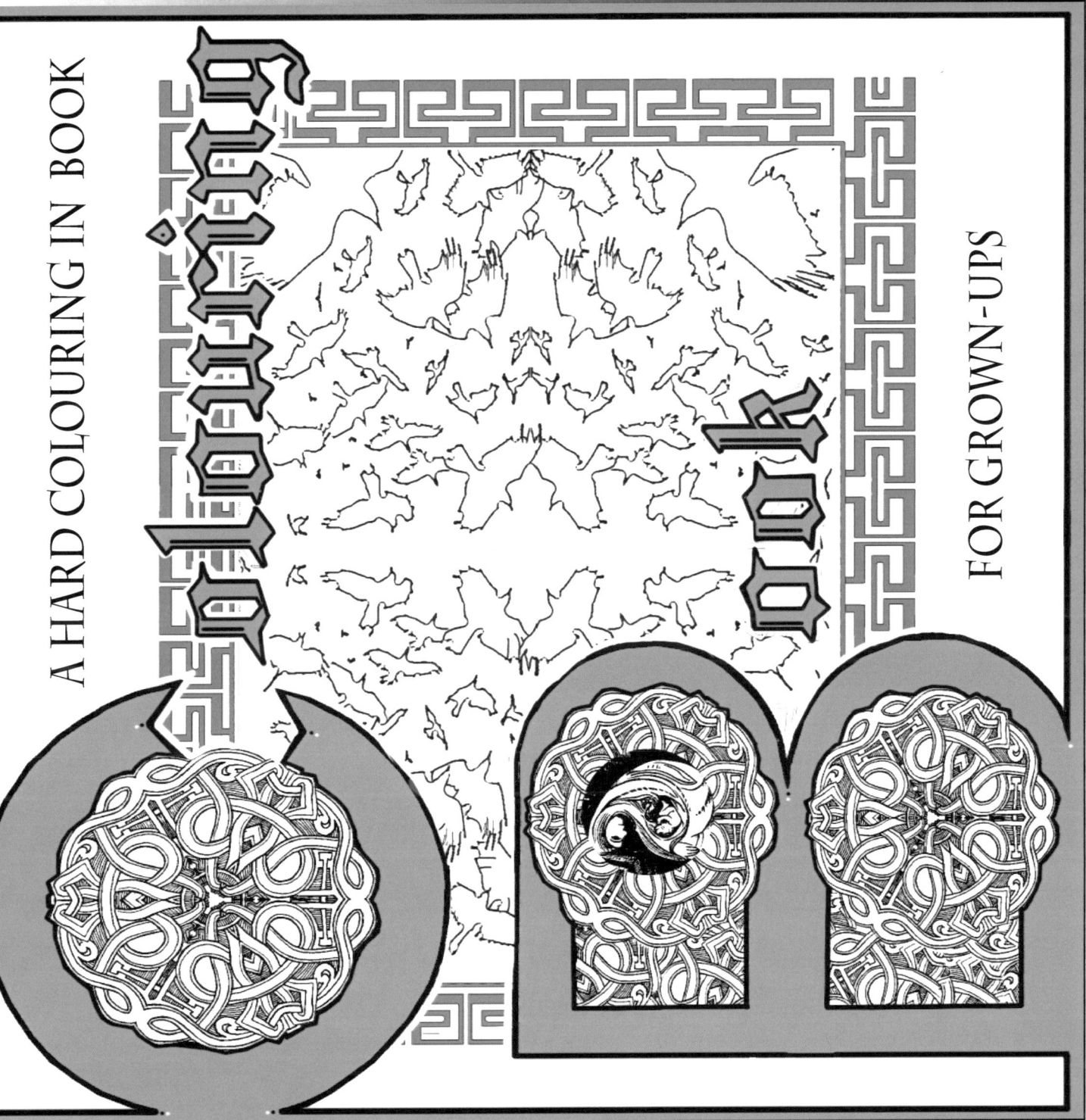

A HARD COLOURING IN BOOK

Colouring book

FOR GROWN-UPS

JOSEPH RICE